Gardening
In Spanish

Useful Spanish Terms and Expressions
for Gardeners, Landscaper Professionals,
Horticulturalists and Produce Growers

by Barbara Thuro

Published by

Ammie Enterprises
P.O. Box 151
Fallbrook, CA 92088-0151
http://ammieenterprises.com/

Gardening In Spanish

English and Spanish

Ammie Enterprises
P.O. Box 151
Fallbrook, CA 92088-0151

1-800-633-5544
Fax: 1-760-451-2096
http://ammieenterprises.com/

ISBN: 093282501X
ISBN-13: 9780932825018

Introduction

This book is offered as an aid to home gardeners, grove managers, farmers, landscapers and anyone else working with a Spanish-speaking employee in the outdoor setting. The following features will assist you in communicating successfully:

Each Spanish word or sentence is followed by a phonetic pronunciation. The syllable **in bold face** receives the accent or stress when pronouncing the word.

Word substitutions can easily be made by using the word lists incorporated into each section or found in the last half of the book. For example, when contracting for services (page..) you want to say "I will pay ____ dollars", simply refer to the Numbers section and complete your sentence.

The use of the Spanish masculine (el) and feminine (la) can sometimes be confusing. Throughout the book the masculine has generally been used. If you should need to use the feminine, you can change most nouns by changing the final vowel to **a** or adding **a** to words ending with a consonant. For example:

Gardener	El Jardinero (masculine)
	El Jardinera (feminine)
Buyer	El Comprador(masculine)
	La Compradora (feminine)

The Spanish language utilizes two forms of address, the familiar and the formal. The familiar is used in family situations, with close friends, and with children. The formal is used in addressing employees and is used throughout this book.

Most sentence patterns are in the "command" form. (For example "Put the dirt over there.") Using the word **please** and a pleasant voice tone or a smile will go a long way in softening the abruptness of the command form.

Every worker, regardless of job responsibility needs to know when the job is being performed well. For that reason, the Expressions of Courtesy section has sentence patterns that will assist you in complimenting your workers. This is especially important when there is a language barrier and there may be concern as to whether instructions were understood.

Vocabulary and sentence patterns for use of chemical pesticides and herbicides have not been included in this text. One must be aware of the dangers and liabilities of using such products before subjecting employees to chemical risks and hazards. Further information can be obtained from your local agriculture department.

It is suggested that you read through the text and familiarize yourself with the location of each topic so that it can be readily located when needed.

PRONUNCIATION GUIDE

Spanish Vowels............................ English Pronunciation

a .... "ah" as in father
e (when ending a syllable).............. "eh" as in let
e (when a syllable ends in a consonant) ... "ay" as in say
i... "ee" as in see
o .... "oh" as in open
u .... "oo" as in moon
u is silent when preceeded by q (que = keh)

Spanish Consonants .... English Pronunciation

c (followed by a, o, u).................... "k" as in come
c (followed by e, i) .... "s" as in this
g (followed by a, o, u) .... "g" as in get
g (followed by e, i) .... "h" as in hot
h .... silent
j... "h" as in has
ll (like English y).......................... "y" as in yet
ñ .... "ny" as in canyon
qu (followed by e, i)....................... "k" as in king
rr .... trilled
v .... "b" as in boy
z .... "s" as in sun
y (is the Spanish word for "and") "ee" as in see

Spanish Accents

Most words ending in a consonant, except for n or s, are stressed on the last syllable (example: juventud, professor).

Most words ending in a vowel or n or s have the stress on the next to the last syllable (example: clase, pantalones)

Words not pronounced according to these rules will have an accent mark on the syllable to be stressed (example: lección, triángulo).

Contracting
For
Services

Contracting for Services

Do you speak any English? ....¿Habla algo inglés?
AH-BLAH **AHL**-GO EN-**GLEHS**?

I don't speak much Spanish. ......No hablo mucho español.
NO **AH**-BLOH **MOO**-CHOH
ES-PAHN-**YOHL.**

Do you understand me? ....¿Me entiende?
MEH EN-TEE-**EHN**-DEH?

What is your name? ....¿Como se llama usted?
KOH-MOH SEH **YAH**-MAH
OO-**STED**?

My name is _____ ....Me llamo _____.
MEH **YAH**-MO_____.

Can you work <u>today</u>?...............¿Puede trabajar <u>hoy</u>?
POO-**EH**-DEH TRA-BAH-**HAR**
<u>OH-EE</u>?

(Substitutions for <u>today</u>:)
  all day...........................todo el día
  TOH-DOH EL **DEE**-AH

  more than one day.............más de un día
  MAHS DEH OON **DEE**-AH

  tomorrow ....mañana
  MAH-**NYA**-NAH

tomorrow morning ....mañana por la mañana
MAH-**NYA**-NAH POHR LA
MAH-**NYA**-NAH

tomorrow afternoon..........mañana por la tarde
MAH-**NYA**-NAH POHR LA
TAR-DEH

day after tomorrow ....pasado mañana
PAS-**SAH**-DO MAH-**NYA**-NAH

this week ....esta semana
EHS-TAH SHE-**MAH**-NAH

this month ....este mes
EHS-TEH MEHS

once a week ....una vez por semana
OOH-NAH VEHS POHR
SEH-**MAH**-NAH

every Sunday ....Cada domingo
CAH-DAH DOH-**MEEN**-GOH

Monday ....lunes
LOO-NEHS

Tuesday.........................martes
MAHR-TES

Wednesday......................miércoles
MEE-**EHR**-KOH-LES

Thursday ....jueves
                                HOO-**EH**-VES

Friday............................viernes
                                VEE-**EHR**-NES

Saturday ....sábado
                                SAH-BAH-DOH

for _____ hours ....por_____horas
                                POHR_____**OH**-RAS

How long can you work? ....¿Cuánto tiempo puede trabajar?
                                KUAHN-TOH TEE-**EHM**-POH
                                POO-**EH**-DEH TRA-BAH-**HAR**?

What do you charge per hour? ...¿Cuánto cobra por hora?
                                KOOAHN-TOH **KOH**-BRAH
                                POHR **OH**-RAH

(day) ....(día)
                                  (**DEE-**AH)

(week)...........................(semana)
                                  (SEH-**MAH**-NAH)

I will pay you _____ dollars......Pago_____ dolares.
                                PAH-GO_____**DOH**-LA-RES

an hour ....por hora
                                POHR **OH**-RAH

a day ....por día
                                POHR **DEE**-AH

a week ....por semana
                          POHR SEH-**MAH**-NAH

The pay is by the... ....El pago es por
                          EL **PAH**-GO EHS POHR

box ....caja
                          KAH-HAH

tray ....bandeja
                          BAHN-**DEH**-HAH

row ....hilera
                          EE-**LEH**-RAH

vine ....planta trepadora
                          PLAHN-TAH
                          TREH-PAH-**DOH**-RAH

Your pay includes lunch. ....Su pago inluye lonche
                          (almuerzo).
                          SOO **PAH**-GO EEN-
                          KLOO-YEH **LOHN**-CHE
                          (AHL-**MOOEHR**-SOH).

Your pay does not include meals. ...Su pago no incluye comida.
                          SOO **PAH**-GOH EEN-**KLOO**-YEH
                          KOH-**MEE**-DAH.

I'd like you to start now............Quiero que empiece ahora.
                          KEE-**EH**-ROH KEH EHM-PEE-**EH**-
                          SEH AH-**OH**-RAH.

Your day will end at ____o'clock. ...... Su día de trabajo terminará a las ___.

SOO **DEE**-A TRAH-**BAH**-HOH

TEHR-MEE-NAHR-**AH** AH LAS ___.

I need your service for one.......... Necesito sus servicios por un....

NEH-SEH-**SEE**-TOH SOOS SEHR-

VEE-SEEOHS POR OON...

Day ....día

DEE-AH

Week ....semana

SEH-**MAH**-NAH

Month ....mes

MEHS

What is your address? ....¿Cual es su direccion?

KOOAHL ES SOO

SEE-REK-**SEEOHN?**

Do you have a telephone? ....¿Tiene teléfono?

TEE-**EH**-NEH TEH-**LEH**-FOH NO?

What is your telephone number?... ¿Cual es su número de teléfono?

KOOAHL ES SOO **NOO**-MEH-

ROH DEH TEH-**LEH**-FOH-NO?

Please write down your........... Escriba, por favor, su.....

ES-**KREE**-BAH, POR FAH-**VOR**,

SOO...

Name ....Nombre

NOHM-BREH

Address...........................Direccion
                                 DEE-REK-SEE-**OHN**

Phone Number ....Número de teléfono
                                 NOO-MEH-ROH DEH
                                 TEH-**LEH**-FOH-NO

Social Security Number ......Número de seguro social
                                 NOO-MEH-ROH DEH SEH-**GOO**-
                                 ROH SO-SEE-**AHL**

I cannot pay you unless you have   No le puedo pagar sin su
your social security number. .... número de seguro social.
                                 NO LE **POOEH**-DOH PAH-**GAR**
                                 SEEN SOO **NOO**-MEH-ROH DEH
                                 SEH-**GOO-**ROH SO-SEE-**AHL.**

Where are you from? ....¿De dondé viene?
                                 DEH **DOHN**-DEH VEE-**EH**-NEH?

Is your family with you? ....¿Está aquí su familia?
                                 EH-**STAH** AH-**KEE**
                                 FAH-**MEE**-LEEAH?

How many are in your family?....¿Cuantos hay en su familia?
                                 KOO-**AHN**-TOHS AEE EN SOO
                                 FAH-**MEE**-LEEAH?

What kind of work do you do?...... ¿Que tipo de trabajo puede hacer?
                                 KEH **TEE**-POH DEH TRAH-**BAH**-
                                 HOH POO-**EH**-DE AH-**SEHR?**

I want to hire you to.................. Quiero emplearlo a usted para.....
KEE-**EH**-ROH EHM-PLEH-**AR**-
LOH AH OO-**STED PAH**-RAH...

clean up the yard ....limpiar el patio.
LEEM-PEE-**AHR** EL PAH-**TEEOH.**

plant............................plantar...
PLAHN-**TAR...**

mow the lawn. ....cortar el césped.
KOHR-**TAR** EL SES-PED.

pack... ....empacar...
EHM-**PAH**-KAR...

pick............................escoger...
EHS-KOH-**HEHR...**

trim trees.....................podar árboles...
POH-**DAR AR**-BOH-LEHS...

build fences.....................construir cercas.
KOHN-STROO-**EER SEHR**-KAHS.

lay bricks. ....colocar ladrillos.
KOH-LOH-**KAR** LAH-**DREE-**YOS.

put in an irrigation system. ...poner un sistema de irrigación.
POH-**NEHR** OON-
SEE-**STEH**-MAH DEH
EE-REE-GAH-SEE-**OHN.**

dig trenches....................cavar trincheras.
                                KAH-**VAR** TREEN-**CHEH**-RAS.

pull weeds. ....sacar la hierba mala
                                SAH-**KAHR** LAH EE-**EHR**-BAH
                                MAH-LA.

lay sod. ....poner terrón .
                                POH-**NEHR** TEH-**ROHN.**

drive a tractor. ....manejar un tractor.
                                MAH-NEH-**HAR** OON
                                TRAK-TOR.

drive a truck on a public road.   manejar un camión público en un
                                camino público.
                                MAH-NEH-**HAR** OON KAH-MEE-
                                OHN EHN OON KAH-**MEE**-OHN
                                POO-BLEE-KOH.

Do you have a drivers License?...¿Tiene licencia para manejar?
                                TEE-**EH**-NEH LEE-**SEN**-SEEAH
                                PAH-RAH MAN-EH-**HAR?**

May I see it? ....¿Puedo verla?
                                POOEH-DOH **VEHR**-LAH?

Notes

_____

_____

_____

_____

_____

_____

_____

_____

_____

_____

_____

_____

_____

_____

_____

Notes

_____

_____

_____

_____

_____

_____

_____

_____

_____

_____

_____

_____

_____

_____

Giving
Directions

General Directions

Please come over here. ....Venga aquí, por favor.
VEHN-GAH AH-**KEE,** POHR
FAH-**VOHR**.

Come in. ....Pase usted.
PAH-SEE OO-**STED**.

This way please......................Por aquí por favor.
POHR AH-**KEE** POHR FAH-**VOR**.

Put your things here (there). .....Ponga sus cosas aquí (allí).
POHN-GAH SOOS **KOH**-SAHS
AH-**KEE** (AH-**YEE**).

I am in charge. ....Soy el jefe (patron).
SOY EL **HEH**-FEH (PAH-**TROHN**).

This is a non-smoking area. ....Se prohibe fumar aquí.
SEH PROH-**EE**-BEH FOO-**MAHR**
AH-**KEE.**

I prefer that you don't   Prefiero que no fume cuando
smoke on the job ....trabaja.
PREH-FE-**EH**-ROH KEH NOH
FOO-ME **KOOAHN**-DOH
TRAH-**BAH**-HAH.

Drinking alcohol is not   Se prohibe tomar alcohol.
allowed. ....SEH PRO-**HEE**-BEH TOH-**MAR**
AL-KOHL.

The tools are here. ....Las hierramientas están aquí.
LAHS EE-EHR-AH-MEE-**EN**-TAS
EHS-**TAHN** AH-**KEE.**

The equipment is there. ....El equipo está allí.
EL EH-**KEE**-POH EHS-**TAH**
AH-**YEE.**

Are you ready to start? ....¿Está listo para empezar?
EHS-**TAH LEES**-TOH **PAH**-RAH
EHM-PEH-**SAHR**?

Do you understand?................¿Entiende?
EHN-TEE-**EHN**-DEH?

I'll meet you at the................Lo encuentro en el (la).....
LOH EHN-**KOOEHN**-TROH EHN
EL (LAH)…

I want you to do something   Quiero que haga algo
else now. ....más ahora.
KEE-**EH**-ROH KEH **AH**-GAH
AHL-GO MAHS AH-**OH**-RAH.

I'll be back soon. ....Vuelvo en seguida.
VOO-**EHL**-VOH EHN
SEG-**EE**-DAH.

Rest for awhile. ....Descanse un rato.
DES-**KAHN**-SEH OON
RAH-TOH.

If you break something please
don't be afraid to tell me. ....

Si quebra algo no tenga miedo
avisarme.

SEE-**KEH**-BRAH **ALL**-GO,
NO **TEN**-GAH MEE-**EH**-DO
AH-VEE-**SAR**-MEH.

Do you understand?...............

¿Entiende?

EHN-TEE-**EHN**-DEH?

Do you know which plants
are weeds? ....

¿Sabe cuales de las plantas son
hierbas malas?

SAH-BEH **KOOAH**-LES DEH
LAHS **PLAHN**-TAS SOHN EE-
EHR-BAHS **MAH**-LAHS?

Can you see the weeds in that
bed (area,lawn)? ....

¿Puede ver las hierbas en aquel
era (área, césped)?

POO-**EH**-DEH LAHS EE-**EHR**-
BAHS **MAH**-LAHS EHN AH-
KEHL **EH**-RAH (**AH**-REAH,
SEHS-PEHD)?

Please pull the weeds in
this bed. ....

Saque las hierbas malas de esta
era, por favor.

SAH-KEH LAHS EE-**EHR**-BAHS
MAH-LAHS DEH **EHS**-TAH **EH**-
RAH, POR **FAH**-VOHR.

You can use this tool for
the weeding. ....

Puede usar esta hierramienta
para escardar.

POO-**EH**-DEH OO-**SAHR EHS**-
TAH EE-EHR-RAH-MEE-**EHN**-TA
PAH-RAH EHS-KAHR-**DAHR**.

Be sure to pull the weeds out   Asegurese de sacar las hierbas
by the roots. ....malas por las raices.

AH-SEH-**GOO**-REH-SEH DEH
SAH-**KAHR** LAHS EE-**EHR**-
BAHS **MAH**-LAHS POHR LOHS
RAH-**EE**-SEHS.

Please try to reach the   Trate de alcanzar las hierbas
weeds without walking   malas sin caminar en las eras,
on the beds. ....por favor.

TRAH-TEH DEH AHL-KAHN-
SAHR LAHS EE-**EHR**-BAHS
MAH-LAHS SEEN KAH-MEE-
NAHR EHN LAHS **EH**-RAS, POHR
FAH-**VOHR.**

Put the weeds in....................Ponga las hierbas malas en....

POHN-GAH LAHS EE-**EHR**-BAHS
MAH-LAHS EHN...

the bucket ....el balde

EHL **BAHL**-DEH

the wheelbarrow ....la carretilla

LAH KAH-REH-**TEE**-YAH

the compost pile...............la pila de compuestos

LAH **PEE**-LAH DEH
KOHM-**POOEHS**-TOHS

the trash can...................el basurero

EL BAH-SOO-**REH**-ROH

the bag...........................la bolsa

Do you understand?................¿Entiende?
                                 EHN-TEE-**EHN**-DEH?

Raking

Here is the rake. ....Aquí está el rastrillo.
                                 AH-**KEE** EH-**STAH** EL
                                 RAHS-**TREE**-YOH.

The rake is in the shed. ....El rastrillo está en la cabaña .
                                 EHL RAHS-**TREE**-YOH EH-**STAH**
                                 EHN LAH KAH-**BAH**-NYAH.

Please rake the leaves from   Rastrille las hojas de este area,
this area.............................por favor.
                                 RAHS-**TREE**-YEH LAHS **OH**-HAHS
                                 DEH **EHS**-TEH **AH**-REAH, POHR
                                 FAH-**VOHR.**

Rake the front (back) yard. ....Rastrille el césped en frente
                                 (detrás) de la casa.
                                 RAHS-**TREE**-YEH EL **SEHS**-PEHD
                                 EHN **FREHN**-TEH (DEH-**TRAHS**)
                                 DEH LAH **KAH**-SAH.

Remove the leaves from the   Saque las hojas de las eras de
flower beds. ....flores.
                                 SAH-KEH LAHS **OH**-HAHS
                                 DEH LAHS **EH**-RAHS DEH
                                 FLOH-REHS.

Be careful not to injure the   Cuidado con dañar las
other plants with the rake..........otras plantas con el rastrillo.
                                        KOOEE-**DAH**-DOH KOHN
                                        DAHN-**YAR** LAHS **OH**-TRAS
                                        PLAHN-TAHS KOHN EL
                                        RAHS-**TREE**-YOH

Please put the leaves in.............Pon las hojas en......

    the trash can.....................el basurero
                                        EL BAH-SOO-**REH**-ROH

    the wheelbarrow ....la carretilla
                                        LAH KAH-REH-**TEE**-YAH

    the compost pile...............la pila compuestos, el montón
                                        de abono
                                        LAH PEE-LAH DEH KOHM-
                                        POOEHS-TOHS, EHL MOHN-
                                        TOHN DEH AH-BOH-NO

    the bag...........................la bolsa
                                        LAH **BOHL**-SAH

Do you understand?................¿Entiende?
                                        EHN-TEE-**EHN**-DEH?

Mowing and Edging
Do you know how to use the   ¿Sabe como usar la cortadora
lawn mower? ....de césped?
                                        SAH-BEH **KOH**-MOH OO-**SAR**
                                        LAH KOR-TAH-**DOH**-RAH DEH
                                        SEHS- PED?

The lawn mower is in the shed. ...La cortadora está en la cabaña.

LAH KOR-TAH-**DOR**-AH EHS-

TAH EHN LAH KAH-**BAH**-NYAH.

I'll show you how to start the ....Le mostraré como empezar la
mower. ....segadora.

LEH MOS-TRAR-**EH KOH**-

MOH EHM-PEH-**SAR** LAH

SEH-GAH-**DOH**-RAH.

I'll work with you until   Trabajaré con usted hasta que
I'm sure you know how to   este seguro que entiendo como
use it. ....usarlo.

TRAH-BAH-HAR-**EH** KOHN

OO-**STED AHS**-TAH KEH

EHS-**TEH** SEH-**GOO**-ROH KEH

EHN-TEE-**EHN**-DEH **KOH**-MOH

OO-**SAR**-LO.

Please mow the lawn...............Corte el césped, por favor.

KOR-TEH EL **SEHS**-PEHD, POR

FAH-**VOR**

Do you know how to use the   ¿Sabe como usar la máquina
edger? ....para cortar el borde?

SAH-BEH **KOH**-MOH OO-**SAR**

LAH **MAH**-KEE-NAH **PAH**-RAH

KOHR-**TAR** EL **BOR**-DEH?

I'll show you how to use the   Le mostraré como usar la má
edger. ....quina para cortar el borde.

LEH MOHS-TRAR-**EH KOH**-

MOH OO-**SAR** LAH **MAH**-KEE-

NAH **PAH**-RAH KOHR-**TAR** EL

BOR-DEH.

Please edge around the lawn......Corte alrededor de la césped,
por favor.
KOR-TEH AHL-REH-DEH-
DOR DEH LA **SEHS**-PEHD POR
FAH-**VOR.**

Be careful not to injure the ....Cuidado con dañar las plantas.
plants. ....KOOEE-**DAH**-DOH KOHN
DAHN-**YAR** LAHS **PLAHN**-TAHS.

Please rake after mowing   Rastrille después de segar y
and edging. ....cortar por favor.
RAH-**STREE**-YEH DEHS-**POOEHS**
DEH SEH-**GAHR** EE **KOHR**-
TAHR. POHR FAH-**VOHR.**

Please sweep the patio and the   Barra el patio y la entrada
entry way when you finish. ....cuando termina por favor.
BAR-RAH EL **PAH**-TEEOH EE LA
EN-**TRAH**-DAH KOO-**AHN**-DOH
TEHR-**MEE**-NAH POR FAH-**VOR.**

Do you understand?...............¿Entiende?
EHN-TEE-**EHN**-DEH?

Preparing the Soil
Use this shovel. ....Use esta pala.
OO-SEH **EHS**-TAH **PAH**-LAH.

Dig a hole here......................Cave un hoyo aquí.
KAH-VEH OON **OH**-YOH
AH-**KEE.**

Make it _____ inches deep. .... Cávelo_____pulgadas de
profundidad.
KAH-VEH-LOH___
POOL-**GAH**-DAHS DEH
PRO-FOON-DEE-**DAHD**.

Dig a ditch from here to there.... Cave una zanja desde aquí hasta
allí.
KAH-VEH **OO**-NAH **SAHN**-HAH
DEHS-DEH AH-**KEE AH**-STAH
AH-**YEE**.

Make it _____ feet long   Cávela_____pies de largo
and _____feet wide................ y _____pies de ancho.
KAH-VEH-LAH___PEEHS DEH
LAR-GOH EE___PEEHS DEH
AHN-CHOH.

It needs to be longer (wider,   Necesita ser más largo
deeper). .... (ancho,hondo).
NEH-SEH-**SEE**-TAH SEHR MAHS
LAR-GOH (**AHN**-CHOH,
OHN-DOH).

Put the dirt here (there). .... Pongo la tierra aquí (allí).
POHN-GAH LAH TEE-**EH**-RAH
AH-**KEE** (AH-**YEE**).

Mix the fertilizer into the soil. ... Mezcle el abono con la tierra.
MEHS-KLEH EL AH-**BOH**-NO
KOHN LAH TEE-**EH**-RAH.

Turn the soil over. .... Remueva la tierra.
REH-**MOOEH**-VAH LAH
TEE-**EH**-RAH.

Do you know how to... ....¿Sabe como........
                                          SAH-BEH **KOH**-MOH...

  use the plow?..................usar el arado?
                                          OO-**SAR** EL AH-**RAH**-DOH?

  use the cultivator? ....usar el cultivador?
                                          OO-**SAR** EL
                                          KOOL-TEE-VAH-**DOR?**

  drive the tractor? ....manejar el tractor?
                                          MAHN-EH-**HAR** EL
                                          TRAHK-TOR?

  arrange the plastic?............arreglar el plástico?
                                          AH-REH-**GLAR** EL
                                          PLAHS-TEE-KOH?

This is where you turn the   Aquí está donde poner en
machine on. ....marcha la maquina.
                                          AH-KEE ES-**TAH** DOHN-**DEH**
                                          POH-**NEHR** EHN-**MAR**-CHAH
                                          LAH **MAH**-KEE-NAH.

Do you understand?...............¿Entiende?
                                          EHN-TEE-**EHN**-DEH?

Planting
Today we are going to   Hoy vamos a plantar.....
plant_____. ....OEE **VAH**-MOHS AH
                                          PLAHN-TAR_____.

Plant the seeds in a row
from here to there. ....Plante las semillas en una hilera
desde aquí hasta allí.

PLAHN-TEH LAHS SEH-**MEE**-
YAHS EHN **OO**-NAH EE-**LEH**-RAH
DEHS-DEH AH-**KEE AHS**-TAH
AY-**YEE.**

Plant the tree (plant) in
this hole..............................Plante el arbol (la planta) en
este hoyo.

PLAHN-TEH EL **AR**-BOHL (LAH
PLAHN-TAH) EHN **EHS**-TEH
OH-YOH.

Plant them_____ inches deep....Plántelos____pulgadas de
profundidad.

PLAHN-TEH-LOHS___
PUHL-**GAH**-DAHS DEH
PROH-FOON-DEE-**DAHD.**

Put the fertilizer in the hole
and mix it with the soil before
you plant. ....Ponga el fertilizante en el hoyo
y mézclelo con la tierra antes
de plantar.

POHN-GAH EL FEHR-TEE-LEE-
SAHN-THE EHN EL **OH**-YOH EE
MEHS-KLEH-LOH KOHN LAH
TEE-**EH**-RAH **AHN**- TEHS DEH
PLAHN-TAR.

Put some water in the hole
before you plant. ....Ponga un poco de agua en el
hoyo antes de plantar.

POHN-GAH OON **POH**-KOH
DEH **AH**-GOOAH EHN EL
OH-YOH **AHN**-TEHS DEH
PLAHN-TAR.

Please water the soil after   Moje la tierra después de
you plant. ....plantar por favor.

> **MOH**-HEH LA TEE-**EH**-RAH
> DEHS-**POOEHS** DEH **PLAHN**-
> TAR POR FAH-**VOR.**

Put the plastic (mulch)   Ponga el plástico (estiércol)
around the plants ....alrededor de las plantas.

> **POHN**-GAH EL **PLAH**-STEE-
> KOH (EHS-TEE-**EHR**-KOHL)
> AHL-REH-DEH-**DOHR** DEH LAS
> **PLAHN**-TAHS.

Stretch the plastic from   Extienda el plástico desde
here to there. ....aquí hasta allí..

> EKS-TEE-**EHN**-DAH EL **PLAH**-
> STEE-KOH **DEHS**-DEH AH-**KEE**
> **AH-**STAH AH-**YEE.**

Please turn the water on (off). ...Abra (cierre) la llave de agua
                               por favor.

> **AH**-BRAH (SEH-**EH**-REH) LA
> **YAH**-VEH DEH **AH** GOOAH POR
> **FAH**-VOR.

Do you understand?................¿Entiende?

> EHN-TEE-**EHN**-DEH?

Harvesting
Pick (cut) the _____...........Recoja (corte) el (la) _____.

> REH-**KOH**-HAH (**KOR**-TEH) EL
> (LAH)

Use the knife (clippers)............Use el cuchillo (las tijeras).
OO-SEH EL KOO-**CHEE**-YOH
(LAHS TEE-**HEH**-RAS).

Don't pull them off................No los jale.
NO LOHS **HAH**-LEH.

Remove the leaves.................Saque las hojas.
SAH-KEH LAHS **OH**-HAS.

Please put the carefully   Póngalos con cuidado en
back in the box. ....la caja por favor.
POHN-GAH-LOHS KOHN
KOOEE-**DAH**-DOH EN LAH
KAH-HAH, POR FAH-**VOR.**

Don't pick the green   No escoje los que son verdes
(spoiled ones). ....(podridos).
NO EHS-**KOH**-HEH LOHS
KEH SOHN **VEHR**-DEHS
(POH-**DREE**-DOHS).

Put the bad ones here (there).....Ponga los podrinos aquí (allí).
POHN-GAH LOHS POH-**DREE**-
DOHS AH-**KEE** (AH-**YEE**).

Leave the small ones on the tree....Deje los inmaturos en el arbol.
DEH-HEH-LOHS EEN-MAH-**TOO**-
ROHS EN EL **AR**-BOHL.

Put the full boxes... ....Ponga alas cajas llenas...
POHN-GAH LAHS **KAH**-HAS
YEH-NAS

here (there)......................aqui (allí).
A-**KEE** (AH-**YEE**).

in the barn (shed)..............en la granja (cabaña).
EN LAH **GRAHN**-HAH
(KAY-**BAH**-NYAH).

in the back of the truck.......en la parte de atrás del camion
EN LAH **PAR**-TEH DEH AH-
TRAHS DEL KAH-**MEEOHN**

on the loading dock ....en el cargadero
EN EL KAR-GAH-**DEH**-ROH

Please load all the boxes into   Cargue todas las cajas en el
the truck. ....camión por favor.
KAR-GEH **TOH**-DAS LAHS **KAH**-
HAHS EN EL KAH-**MEEOHN** POR
FAH-**VOR.**

You may eat as much fruit as   Puede comer tanta fruta como
you like. ....quiera.
POO-**EH**-DEH KOH-**MEHR**
TAHN-TAH **FROO**-TAH **KOH**-
MOH KEE-**EH**-RAH.

Would you like to take some   ¿Quiere llevar algo de _____ a
extra_____ home with you? ....su casa?
KEE-**EH**-REH YEH-**VAHR**
AHL-GOH DEH ____ AH SOO
KAH-SAH?

We have a good (bad) crop
this year. ....
Tenemos una buena (mala)
cosecha este año.
TEH-**NEH**-MOHS **OO**-NAH
BOOEH-NAH (**MAH**-LAH) KOH-
SEH-CHAH EHS-**TEH AHN**-YOH.

That's all for now...................
Es todo por ahora.
ES **TOH**-DOH POR AH-**OH**-RAH.

Cleaning Up
Please put the trash in a
plastic bag. ....
Ponga la basura en una bolsa de
plástico, por favor.
POHN-GAH LAH BAH-**SOO**-
RAH EN **OO**-NA **BOHL**-SAH
DEH **PLAHS**-TEE-KOH, POR
FAH-**VOR**.

We're going to burn the
brush. Put it in a pile
over there. ....
Vamos a quemar el breñal.
Pongalo en un montón allá.
VAH-MOHS AH KEH-**MAR** EL
BREH-**NYAHL**. **POHN**-GAH-LOH
EN OON MOHN **TOHN** AH-**YAH**

Empty the contents of the
wheelbarrow into the trash
can (compost pile). ....
Ponga el contenido de la
carretilla en el basurero
(pila de compuestos).
POHN-GAH EL KOHN-TEE-**NEE**-
DOH DEH LA KAH-REH-**TEE**-
YAH EN EL BAH-SOO-**REH**-ROH
(**PEE**-LAH DEH KOHM-**POOEHS**-
TOHS), POR FAH-**VOR**.

Take the trash cans to the
side (front,back) of the house. ...

Lleve los basureros al lado
(delante de detrás de) la casa.
YEH-VEH LOHS BAH-SOO-**REH**-
ROHS AHL **LAH**-DOH (DEH-
LAHN-TEH DEH, DEH-**TRAHS**
DEH) LAH **KAH**-SAH.

Look around and see if we've
left any tools out. ....

Busque alrededor para ver si
hemos dejado algunas herra-
mientas afuera.
BOOS-KEH AHL-REH-DEH-**DOR**
PAH-RAH VEHR SEE **EH**-MOS
DEH-**HAH**-DOH AHL-**GOO**-
NAHS EHR-AH-MEE-**YEHN**-TOHS
AH-**FOOEH**-RAH POR FAH-**VOR.**

Please put everything back
in the shed. ....

Guarde todas las cosas en la
cabaña, por favor.
GOOARH-DEH **TOH**-DAHS LAHS
KOH-SAHS EN LAH KAH-**BAH**-
NYA, POR FAH-**VOR.**

Close (open) the door (gate) .....

Cierre (abra) la puerta (entrada)
SEE-**EH**-REH (**AH**-BRAH)
LA POO-**EHR**-TAH
(EHN-**TRAH**-DAH),

Do you understand?...............

¿Entiende?
EHN-TEE-**EHN**-DEH?

Ending the Work Period

It's time to stop working...........

Es hora terminar el trabajo.
EHS **OH**-RAH TEHR-MEE-**NAR** EL
TRA-**BAH**-HOH.

It's time to leave. ....Es hora de irse.
EHS **OH**-RAH DEH **EER**-SEH.

Can you come back tomorrow?...¿Puede regresar mañana?
POO-**EH**-DEH REH-GREH-**SAR**
MAH-**NYAH**-NAH?

I'll take you... ....Lo llevaré...
LOH YEH-VAH-**REH...**

home ....a casa
AH **KAH**-SAH

to the corner ....a la esquina
AH LAH EH-**SKEE**-NAH

to the market...................al mercado
AHL MEHR-**KAH**-DOH

to the bus stop ....a la parada de autobuses
AH LAH PAH-**RAH**-DAH DEH
AH-OO-TOH-**BOO**-SES

I need help... ....Necesito ayuda....
NEH-SEH-**SEE**-TOH
AH-**YOO**-DAH...

tomorrow......................mañana
MAH-**NYAH**-NAH

day after tomorrow ....pasado mañana
PAH-**SAH**-DOH MAH-**NYAH**-NAH

next week......................la semana próxima
LAH SEH-**MAH**-NAH
PROK-SEE-MAH

next month ....el mes próxima
EL MEHS **PROK**-SEE-MOH

Can you come on the bus? ....¿Puede venir por autobus?
POO-**EH**-DEH VEH-**NEER** POR
AH-OO-TOH-**BOOS**?

Do you have a car?.................¿Tiene carro?
TEE-**EH**-NEH **KAR**-ROH

I don't need help tomorrow.......No necesito ayuda mañana.
NO NEH-SEH-**SEE**-TOH AH-**YOO**-
DAH MAH-**NYAH**-NAH.

This job is finished.................Este trabajo está terminado.
EH-STEH TRAH-**BAH**-HOH EHS-
TAH TEHR-MEE-**NAH**-DOH.

There is no more work. ....El trabajo se acabó.
EL TRAH-**BAH**-HOH SHE
AH-KAH-**BOH.**

Here is your.......................Aquí está el......
AH-**KEE** EHS-**TAH** EL...

pay ....pago
PAH-GOH

money ....dinero
DEE-**NEH**-ROH

Thanks for doing such a great job. .... Gracias por su buen trabajo.
GRAH-SEE-AHS POR SOO BOOEHN TRAH-**BAH**-HOH.

I'll see you tomorrow. .... Hasta mañana.
AH-STAH MAH-**NYA**-AH.

Good-bye. .... Adios.
AH-**DEEOHS.**

<u>Notes</u>

_____

_____

_____

_____

_____

_____

_____

_____

_____

_____

_____

_____

_____

_____

_____

_____

<u>Notes</u>

_____

_____

_____

_____

_____

_____

_____

_____

_____

_____

_____

_____

_____

_____

_____

Helpful
Expressions

Bathroom and Clean Up

The bathroom is................El cuarto de baño esta...
EL **KOOAR**-TOH DEH **BAH**-
NYOH EHS-**TAH**...

here (there)....................Aquí (allí)
AH-**KEE** (AH-**YEE**)

in the house....................En la casa
EN LA **KAH**-SAH

near the barn (shed) ....cerca de la granja (cabaña)
SEHR-KAH DEH LAH **GRAHN**-
HAH (KAH-**BAH**-NYA)

If you need to use the   Si necesita usar el retrete
toilet, let me know. ....avíseme.
SEE NEH-SEH-**SEE**-TAH OO-
SAR EL REH-**TREH**-TEH
AH-**VEE**-SEH-MEH.

Would you like to wash   ¿Quiere lavarse las
your hands?   manos?
KEE-**EH**-REH LAH-**VAR**-SEH
LAHS **MAH**-NOHS?

There is a faucet (sink) here.......Hay una llave de agua
(un lavamanos) aquí.
AHEE **OOH**-NAH **YAH**-VEH DEH
AH-GOOAH (OON LAH-VAH-
MAHN-OHS) AH-**KEE**.

The bathroom has... ....El cuarto de baño tiene...
EL **KOOAR**-TOH DEH **BAHN**-
YOH TEE-**EH**-NEH...

soap ....jabón
HA-**BOHN**

a shower.......................una ducha
OO-NAH **DOO**-CHA

Water
Here is a container of water.......Aquí está un recipiente de agua.
AH-**KEE** EHS-**TAH** OON REH-SEE-
PEE-**EHN**-TEH DEH **AH**-GOOAH

Do you need more water? ....¿Necesita más agua?
NEH-SEH-**SEE**-TAH MAHS
AH-GOOAH?

You can get a drink here (there)....Puede tomar agua aquí (allí).
P OO-**EH**-DEH **TOH**-MAR **AH**-
GOOAH AH-KEE (AH-**YEE**).

You can get a drink   Puede tomar agua de la
from the hose.......................manguera.
POO-**EH**-DEH **TOH-MAR AH**-
GOOAH DEH LAH
MAHN-**GOOEH**-RAH.

Here is a cup.......................Aquí está una taza.
AH-**KEE** EHS-**TAH OOH**-NAH
TAH-SAH.

Food

It's time to eat....................Es hora de comer.
ES **OH**-RAH DEH KOH-
MEHR.

Are you hungry? ....¿Tiene hambre?
TEE-**EH**-NEH **AHM**-BREH?

Here is your lunch.................Aquí está su almuerzo (el
lonche).
AH-**KEE** EHS-**TAH SOO**
AHL-**MOOER**-SOH (EL
LOHN-CHEH).

You can eat here... ....Puede comer aquí...

   on the porch....................en el portal
   EN EL POR-**TAHL**

   on the patio....................en el patio
   EN EL **PAH**-TEEOH

   under the tree.................bajo el arbol
   BAH-HOH EHL **AHR**-BOHL

   over there......................allá
   AH-**YAH**

Have you finished?.................¿Ha terminado?
AH TEHR-MEE-**NAH**-DOH?

Did you have enough to eat?......¿Tenía bastante para comer?
TEH-**NEE**-AH BAH-**STAHN**-TEH
PAH-RAH KOH-**MEHR?**

Safety and First Aid

Please be careful	Tenga cuidado, por favor.
	TEN-GAH KOOEE-**DAH**-DOH,
	POR FAH-**VOR**.

If you hurt yourself let me know right away................	Si se lastima avíseme inmediatamente.
	SEE SEH LAS-**TEE**-MAH AH-**VEE**-
	SEH-MEH EEN-MEH-DEE-AH-
	TAH-**MEHN**-TEH.

Did you hurt yourself?.............	¿Se lastimó?
	SEH LAHS-TEE-**MOH**?

You have a bad cut.................	Tiene una mala cortadura.
	TEE-**EH**-NEH **OO**-NAH **MAH**-
	LAH KOR-TAH-**DOO**-RAH.

I'm going to wash your cut.	Voy a lavar la cortadura.
	VOH-EH AH LAH-**VAR** LAH
	KOR-TAH-**DOO**-RAH.

Here is a bandage.	Aquí hay una curita.
	AH-**KEE** AEE **OOH**-NAH
	KOO-**REE**-TAH.

Do you feel ill?......................	¿Se siente mal?
	SEH SEE-**EHN**-TEH MAHL?

What happened?	¿Que pasó?
	KEH PAH-**SOH**

You need to see a doctor...........	Necesita ver un doctór.
	NEH-SEH-**SEE**-TAH VEHR OOHN
	DOK-**TOR**.

I'm taking you to the hospital. ... Voy a llevarlo al hospital.
VOHY AH YEH-**VAR**-LOH AHL
OHS-PEE-**TAHL.**

I'm taking you home. .... Voy a llevarlo a casa.
VOH-EH AH YEH-**VAR**-LOH AH
KAH-SAH.

Is your family home? .... ¿Está su familia en casa?
EH-**STAH** SOO FAH-**MEE**-LEEAH
EHN **KAH**-SAH?

Where can I take you? .... ¿Adonde puedo llevarlo?
AH-**DOHN**-DEH **POOEH**-DOH
YEH-**VAHR**-LOH?

You are covered by   Mi seguro lo cubre a usted.
my insurance........................ MEE SEH-**GOO**-ROH LOH **KOO**-
BREH AH **OO**-STED.

You will need an x-ray. .... Va a necesitar una radiografía.
VAH AH NEH-SEH-
SEE-**TAR OO**-NAH
RAH-DEE-OH-GRAH-**FEE**-AH.

Do you understand? .... ¿Entiende?
EN-TEE-**EHN**-DEH?

Terminology
Accident .... accidente
AHK-SEE-**DEN**-TEH

Ambulance .... ambulancia
AHM-BOO-**LAHN**-SEEAH

Claim ....demanda
                            DEH-**MAHN**-DAH

Cold ....catarro
                            KAH-**TAH**-ROH

Disability............................incapacidad
                            EEN-KAH-PAH-SEE-**DAHD**

Doctor..............................doctor
                            DOK-**TOR**

Fever................................fiebre
                            FEE-**EH**-BREH

Headache...........................dolor de cabeza
                            DOH-**LOR** DEH KAH-
                            BEH-SAH

Insurance...........................seguro
                            SEH-**GOO**-ROH

Nurse ....enfermera
                            EN-FEHR-**MEH**-RAH

Pain ....dolor
                            DOH-**LOR**

Pill ....píldora
                            PEEL-DOH-RAH

Prescription ....receta
                            REH-**SEH**-TAH

Splinter ....astilla
AHS-**TEE**-YAH

Sick ....enfermo
EN-**FEHR**-MOH

Stomach ache........................dolor de estómago
DOH-**LOR** DEH
EHS-**TOH**-MAH-GO

Swollen...............................hinchado
EEN-**CHAH**-DOH

Toothache ....dolor de muelas
DOH-**LOR** DEH **MOOEH**-LAHS

x-ray ....radiografía
RAH-DEE-OH-GRA-**FEE**-AH

Expressions of Courtesy and Other Helpful Expressions

Good morning......................Buenos días.
BOOEH-NOHS **DEE**-AHS.

Good afternoon.....................Buenas tardes.
BOOEH-NAHS **TAR**-DEHS.

Good evening........................Buenas noches.
BOOEH-NAHS **NO**-CHEHS.

How are you?........................¿Como está usted?
KOH-MOH EHS-**TAH** OO-**STED?**

I'm fine thank you and you? ...... Bien gracias¿Y usted?
                                   BEE-**EHN GRAH**-SEEAHS. EE
                                   OO-**STED?**

Yes. No .... Si. No.
                                   SEE. NO.

Please .... Por favor.
                                   POHR FAH-**VOR.**

Thank you........................... Gracias.
                                   GRAH-SEE-AHS.

You're welcome..................... De nada.
                                   DEH **NAH**-DAH.

Excuse me. .... Perdóneme.
                                   PEHR-**DOHN**-EH-MEH.

I don't understand, please   No entiendo. Hable más
speak more slowly. .... despacio, por favor.
                                   NO EN-TEE-**EN**-DOH. **AH**-BLEH
                                   MAHS DEH-**SPAH**-SEEOH, POR
                                   FAH-**VOR.**

Please repeat........................ Repita por favor.
                                   REE-PEE-TAH POHR FAH-**VOR.**

You're a good worker. .... Usted es un buen trabajador.
                                   OO-**STED** EHS OOHN BOOEN
                                   TRAH-BAH-HAH-**DOR.**

Well done. .... Bien hecho.
                                   BEE-**EHN EH**-CHO.

Excellent work......................Excelente trabajo.
EK-SEH-**LEN**-TEH TRAH-
BAH-HOH.

That's coming along nicely. ....Eso está resultando muy bien.
EH-SOH EH-**STAH** REH-SOOHL-
TAHN-DOH MOOEE BEE-**EN.**

Keep up the good work............Siga adelante con su buen
trabajo.
SEE-GAH AH-DEH-**LAHN**-
TEH KOHN SOO BOOEHN
TRAH-**BAH**-HOH.

I don't know. ....No se.
NO SHE.

Sorry. ....Lo siento.
LOH SEE-**EN**-TOH.

Don't worry. ....No se preocupe.
NO SEH PREH-OH-**KOO**-PEH.

It's hot today would you like   Hace calor hoy. ¿Quiere...
a cold drink?.......................una bebida fria?
OOH-NAH BEH-**BEE**-DAH
FREE-AH?

to take a break? ....descansar un rato?
DEHS-KAHN-**SAR** OON **RAH**-TOH?

to get out of the   salir del so un rato?
sun for awhile? ....SAH-**LEER** DEL SOHL OON
RAH-TOH?

I'd like to have you   Quiero que trabajo aquí
work for me again. ....otra vez.

> KEE-**EH**-ROH KEH TRAH-**BAH**-
> HEH AH-**KEE OH**-TRAH VEHS.

See you tomorrow. ....Hasta mañana.

> **AH**-STAH MAHN-**YAH**-NAH.

Good-bye. ....Adios.

> AH-**DEEOHS.**

See you later. ....Hasta luego.

> **AH**-STAH LOO-**EH**-GOH.

Notes

_____

_____

_____

_____

_____

_____

_____

_____

_____

_____

_____

_____

_____

_____

_____

Word Lists

Numbers
Cardinal Numbers

One .... uno
OOH-NOH

Two .... dos
DOHS

Three .... tres
TREHS

Four .... cuatro
KOOAH-TROH

Five .... cinco
SEEN-KOH

Six .... seis
SEH-EES

Seven .... siete
SEE-**EH**-TEH

Eight .... ocho
OH-CHOH

Nine .... nueve
NOO-**EH**-VEH

Ten .... diez
DEE-**EHS**

Eleven ....once
                                     OHN-SEH

Twelve...............................doce
                                     DOH-SEH

Thirteen.............................trece
                                     TREH-SEH

Fourteen ....catorce
                                     KAH-**TOR**-SEH

Fifteen ....quince
                                     KEEN-SEH

Sixteen ....diez y seis
                                     DEE-**EHS** EE **SEH**-EES

Seventeen ....diez y siete
                                     DEE-**EHS** EE SEE-**EH**-TEH

Eighteen............................diez y ocho
                                     DEE-**EHS** EE **OH**-CHOH

Nineteen ....diez y nueve
                                     DEE-**EHS** EE NOO-**EH**-VEH

Twenty ....viente
                                     VEE-**EN**-TEH

Thirty................................treinta
                                     TREH-**EEN**-TAH

Forty...................................cuarenta
KOOAH-**REN**-TAH

Fifty....................................cincuenta
SEEN-**KOOEN**-TAH

Sixty ....sesenta
SEH-**SEN**-TAH

Seventy ....setenta
SEH-**TEN**-TAH

Eighty..................................ochenta
OH-**CHEN**-TAH

Ninety ....noventa
NO-**VEN**-TAH

Hundred ....cien
SEE-**EN**

Ordinal
First....................................primero
PREE-**MEH**-ROH

Second................................segundo
SEH-**GOON**-DOH

Third...................................tercero
TEHR-**SEH**-ROH

Fourth ....cuarto
KOOAR-TOH

Fifth.....................................quinto
                                   KEEN-TOH

Time

Minute(s) ....minuto (s)
                                   MEE-**NOO**-TOH (S)

Hour ....hora
                                   OH-RAH

Half hour............................media hora
                                   MEH-DEEAH **OH**-RAH

Day....................................día
                                   DEE-AH

    Morning.......................manaña
                                   MAHN-**YAH**-NAH

    Noon   mediodía
                                   MEH-DEE-OH-**DEE**-AH

    Afternoon.....................tarde
                                   TAR-DEH

    Night...........................noche
                                   NOH-CHEH

  Week ....semana
                                   SEH-**MAH**-NAH

    Sunday ....domingo
                                   DOH-**MEEN**-GOH

Monday.........................lunes
LOO-NES

Tuesday ....martes
MAR-TES

Wednesday....................miércoles
MEE-**EHR**-KOH-LES

Thursday ....jueves
HOOEH-VES

Friday ....vierne
VEE-**EHR**-NES

Saturday ....sábado
SAH-BAH-DOH

Month ....mes
MEHS

January ....enero
EN-**NEH**-ROH

February......................febrero
FEH-**BREH**-ROH

March.........................Marzo
MAR-SOH

April ....abril
AH-**BREEL**

May ....mayo
                              MAI-OH

June ....junio
                              HOO-NEEOH

July............................julio
                              HOO-LEEOH

August ....agosto
                              AH-**GOHS**-TOH

September ....septiembre
                              SEP-TEE-**EHM**-BREH

October ....octubre
                              OHK-**TOO**-BREH

November....................noviembre
                              NOH-VEE-**EHM**-BREH

December....................diciembre
                              DEE-SEE-**EHM**-BREH

Year ....Año
                              AH-NYOH

Spring.........................primavera
                              PREE-MAH-**VEH**-RAH

Summer ....verano
                              VEH-**RAH**-NOH

Fall .... otoño
OH-**TOH**-NYOH

Winter .... invierno
EEN-VEE-**EHR**-NO

Now .... ahora
AH-**OH**-RAH

Tonight .... esta noche
EH-STAH **NO**-CHEH

Last night .... anoche
AH-**NO**-CHEH

Tomorrow .... mañana
MAH-**NYAH**-NAH

Day after tomorrow .... pasado mañana
PAH-**SAH**-DOH MAHN-**YAH**-NAH

In the morning .... por la mañana
POR LAH MAHN-**YAH**-NAH

What time is it? .... ¿Que hora es?
KEH **OH**-RAH ES

It's one o'clock .... Es la una.
ES LA **OOH**-NAH

It's four o'clock .... Son las cuatro.
SOHN LAHS **KOOAH**-TROH

It's early .... Es temperano.
EHS TEM-**PRAH**-NO

It's late .... Es tarde.
ES **TAR**-DEH

People

Boss .... el jefe, el patrón
EL **HEH**-FEH, EL PAH-**TROHN**

Buyer .... el comprador
EL COHM-PRAH-**DOR**

Child .... el niño, la niña
EL **NEE**-NYOH, LA **NEE**-NYAH

Crew .... la cuadrilla
LA KOOAH-**DREE**-YAH

Customer .... el cliente
EL KLEE-**EN**-TEH

Family .... la familia
LA FAH-**MEE**-LEEAH

Father .... el papá
EL PAH-**PAH**

Friend .... el (la) amigo(a)
EL (LA) AH-**MEE**-GOH (GAH)

Gardener .... el jardinero
EL HAR-DEE-**NEH**-ROH

Grower .... el cultivador
         EL KOOL-TEE-VAH-**DOR**

Husband .... el esposo
         EL EHS-**POH**-SOH

Inspector .... el inspector
         EL EEN-SPEK-**TOR**

Man .... el hombre
         EL **OHM**-BREH

Manager .... el administrador
         EL AHD-MEE-NEE-STRAH-**DOR**

Mother .... la mamá

Neighbor .... el vecino
         EL VEH-**SEE**-NO

Owner .... el dueño
         EL **DUEH**-NYOH

Packer .... el empaquetador
         EL EM-PAH-KEH-TAH-**DOR**

Parents .... los padres
         LOHS **PAH**-DRES

People .... la gente
         LA **HEN**-TEH

Seller .... el vendedor
         EL VEN-DEH-**DOR**

Supervisor .... el supervisor
EL SOO-PEHR-VEE-**SOR**

Wife .... la esposa
LA EH-**SPOH**-SAH

Woman .... la mujer
LA MOO-**HEHR**

Worker .... el obrero, el trabajador
EL OH-**BREH**-ROH, EL
TRAH-BAH-HAH- **DOR**

Work Locations

Bank (slope) .... el sesgo
EL **SEHS**-GOH

Barn .... el granero
EL GRAHN-**EH**-ROH

Barnyard .... el corral
EL KOH-**RAHL**

Bed (flower) .... la era (de flores)
LA **EH**-RAH (DEH **FLOH**-REHS)

Bench .... el banco
EL **BAHN**-KOH

Border .... el borde
EL **BOR**-DEH

Building .... el edificio
EL EH-DEE-**FEE**-SEEOH

Camp .... el campamento
EL KAHM-PAH-**MEN**-TOH

Canal................................. el canal
EL KAH-**NAHL**

Cannery .... la fábrica de conservas
LA **FAH**-BREE-KAH DEH
KOHN-**SIR**-VAHS

Cellar .... el sótano, la bodega
EL **SOH**-TAH-NO, LA
BOH- **DEH-** GAH

Compost pile .... la pila de compuestos
LA **PEE**-LA DEH KOHM-
POOEHS-TOHS

Dam.................................. el dique
EL **DEE**-KEH

Deck .... la cubierta
LA KOO-BEE-**EHR**-TAH

Ditch................................. la cuneta
LA KOO-**NEH**-TAH

Dump................................ el depósito de basura
EL DEH-**POH**-SEE-TOH DEH
BAH-**SOO**-RAH

Factory .... la fábrica
LA **FAH**-BREE-KAH

Fence ....la cerca
                                     LA **SEHR**-KAH

Field ....el campo
                                     EL-**KAHM**-POH

Garage...................................el garaje
                                     EL GAH-**RAH**-HEH

Garden ....el jardín
                                     EL HAR-**DEEN**

Garden (vegetable).................el jardín de legumbres
                                     EL HAR-**DEEN** DEH
                                     LEH-**GOOM**-BREHS

Garden flower......................la era de flores
                                     LA **EH**-RAH DEH **FLOH**-REHS

Gate...................................la entrada
                                     LA EN-**TRAH**-DAH

Greenhouse.........................la invernadero
                                     EL EEN-VEHR-NAH-**DEH**-ROH

Grove ....la arboleda
                                     LA AR-BOH-**LEH**-DAH

Hill...................................la colina
                                     LA KOH-**LEE**- NAH

Hole ....el hoyo
                                     EL **OH**-YOH

House..................................la casa
LA **KAH**-SAH

Kitchen..............................la cocina
LA KOH-**SEE**-NAH

Lake...................................el lago
EL **LAH**-GOH

Levee ....el díque
EL **DEE**-KAY

Nursery ....el plantel
EL PLAHN-**TELL**

Office................................la oficina
LA OH-FEE-**SEE**-NAH

Orchard ....la huerta
LA **OOEHR**-TAH

Parking lot ....el estacionamento
EL EH-STAH-SEE-OHN-AH-
MEN-TOH

Path ....la senda, el sendero
LA **SEHN**-DAH, EL
SEN-**DEH**-ROH

Patio ....el patio
EL **PAH**-TEEOH

Plot ....la era
LA **EH**-RAH

Pond .... el estanque de agua
EL ES-**TAN**-KEH DEH **AH**-GOOAH

Pool .... el charco, la piscina
EL **CHAR**-KOH, LA PEE-**SEE**-NAH

Ranch............................... el rancho, la estancía
EL **RAHN**-CHOH, LA ES-**STAHN**-
SEEAH

Ravine .... la barranca
LA BAH-**RAHN**-KAH

River .... el río
EL **REE**-OH

Road .... el camino
EL KAH-**MEE**-NO

Septic tank .... el foso séptico
EL **FOH**-SOH **SEP**-TEE- KOH

Shed................................. el cobertizo, la cabaña
EL KOH-BEHR-**TEE**-SOH, LA
KAH-**BAH**-NYAH

Shed (cattle) .... la tenada
LA TEN-**AH**-DAH

Slaughter house .... el matadero
EL MAH-TAH-**DEH**-ROH

Stall .... el pesebre
EL PEH-**SEH**-BREH

Vineyard ....la viña
                                         LA **VEE**-NYAH

Wood pile...........................el montón de madera
                                         EL MOHN-**TOHN** DEH MAH-
                                         DEH-RAH

Workshop ....el tallar
                                         EL TAH-**YAR**

Yard ....el corral
                                         EL KOH-**RAHL**

Tools Equipment Supplies and Materials

Ax ....la hacha
                                         LA **AH**-CHAH

Bag ....el saco, la bolsa
                                         EL **SAH**-KOH, LA **BOHL**-SAH

Bale ....la bala, el fardo
                                         LAH **BAH**-LAH, EL **FAR**-DOH

Basket................................la canasta
                                         LA KAH-**NAHS**-TAH

Bin ....el arcón
                                         EL AR-**KOHN**

Blower...............................el soplador
                                         EL SOAP-LAH-**DOR**

Board ....la tabla
                                         LA **TAHB**-LAH

Bottle .... la botella
                                       LA BOH-**TEH**-YAH

Box .... la caja
                                       LA **KAH**-HAH

Box cardboard .... el carton
                                       EL KAR-**TOHN**

Bricks .... los ladrillos
                                       LOHS LAH-**DREE**-OHS

Broom .... la escoba
                                       LA ES-**KOH**-BAH

Brush .... el cepillo
                                       EL SEH-**PEE**-YOH

Bucket .... el cubo, el balde
                                       EL **KOO**-BOH, EL **BAHL**-DEH

Bulb .... el bulbo
                                       EL **BUHL**-BOH

Cable .... el cable
                                       EL **KAH**-BLEH

Cage .... la jaula
                                       LA HAH-**OO**-LAH

Can .... la lata
                                       LA **LAH**-TAH

Cart .... la carreta
LA KAH-**REE**-TAH

Cement............................... el cemento
EL SEH-**MEN**-TOH

Cement mixer...................... la mezcladora de cemento
LA MES-KLAH-**DORA** DEH
SEH-**MEN**-TOH

Chain .... la cadena
LA KAH-**DEH**-NAH

Combine .... la segadora
LAH SEH-GAH-**DOH**-RAH

Compost .... los compuestos
LOHS KOHM-**POOHS**-TOHS

Concrete .... el hormigón
EL OR-MEE-**GOHN**

Concrete reinforced .... el hormigón armado
EL OR-MEE-**GOHN** AR-
MAH-DOH

Crate................................. la cesta grande
LA **SEHS**-TAH **GRAHN**-DEH

Cultivator .... el cultivador
EL KOOL-TEE-VAH-**DOR**

Disc .... el disco
EL **DEES**-KOH

Drill.....................................el taladro
EL TAH-**LAH**-DROH

Edger ....la máquina para cortar el borde
LA **MAH**-KEE-NAH **PAH**-RAH
KOR-**TAR** EL **BOR**-DEH

Engine ....el motor
EL MOH-**TOR**

Equipment...........................el equipo, el equipaje
EL EH-**KEE**-POH, EL EH-KEE
PAH-HEH

Fan ....el ventilador
EL VEN-TEE-LAH-**DOR**

Faucet................................la llave de agua
LA **YAH**-VEH DEH **AH**-GUAH

Fence ....la cerca
LA **SEHR**-KAH

Fence post ....el poste
EL **POH**-STEH

Fertilizer ....el fertilizante, el estiércol
EL FEHR-TEE-LEE-**SAHN**-THE, EL
ES-TEE-**EHR**-KOHL

Fruit picker..........................el escogedor de fruta
EL ES-KOH-HEH-**DOR** DEH
FROO-TAH

Funnel .... el ambudo
                    EL EM-**BOO**-DOH

Gas .... la gasolina
                    LA GAH-SOH-**LEE**-NAH

Glass .... el vidrio
                    EL **VEED**-REEOH

Gloves .... los guantes
                    LOHS **GOOAHN**-TES

Goggles.............................. los lentes protectivos
                    LOHS **LEHN**-TEHS PRO-TEK-
                    TEE-VOHS

Gravel .... el cascajo
                    EL KAS-**KAH**-HOH

Grease .... la grasa
                    LA **GRAH**-SAH

Gun .... la pistola
                    LA PEES-**TOH**-LAH

Gypsum .... el yeso
                    EL **YEH**-SOH

Hammer .... el martillo
                    EL MAR-**TEE**-YOH

Handle................................ el mango
                    EL **MAHN**-GOH

Hat . . . . el sombrero
EL SOHM-**BREH**-ROH

Hoe . . . . el azador
EL AH-SAH-**DOR**

Hook . . . . el gancho
EL **GAHN**-CHOH

Hose . . . . la manguera
LA MAHN-**GOOEH**-RAH

Incubator . . . . la incubadora
LA EEN-KO-BAH-**DOH**-RAH

Irrigation system . . . . sistema de irrigación
SEE-**STEH**-MAH DEH EE-REE-
GAH-**SEEOHN**

Jack . . . . la gata
LA **GAH-**TAH

Jug . . . . el jarro
EL **HAH**-ROH

Key . . . . la llave
LA **YAH**-VEH

Knife . . . . el cuchillo
EL KOO-**CHEE**-YOH

Knife large . . . . el machete
EL MAH-**SHEH**-TEH

Ladder . . . . .la escalara de mano
LA ES-KAH-**LEH**-RAH DE
MAH-NOH

Lawn mower . . . . .la cortadora, de césped
LA SEH-GAH-**DOR**-AH, DEH
SES-PED

Liquid. . . . . .el líquido
EL **LEE**-KEE-DOH

Lock . . . . .la cerradura
LA SEH-RAH-**DOO**-RAH

Machine . . . . .la máquina
LA **MAH**-KEE-NAH

Machinery . . . . .la maquinaria
LA MAH-KEE-**NAH**-REE-AH

Manure . . . . .el abono
EL AH-**BOH**-NO

Materials . . . . .los materiales
LOHS MAH-TEH-REE-**AH**- LEHS

Mousetrap . . . . .la ratonera
LA RAH-TOH-**NEH**-RAH

Mower. . . . . .la cortadura, de césped
LA KOR-TAH-**DOO**-RAH, DEH
SES-PED

Mulch......................................el estiércol
EL ES-TEE-**EHR**-KOHL

Nails ....los clavos
LOHS **KLAH**-VOHS

Net......................................la red
LA RED

Nut......................................la tuerca
LA **TOOER**-KAH

Oil ....el aciete
EL AH-SEE-**EH**-TEH

Pail ....el cubo
EL **KOO**-BOH

Paint ....la pintura
LA PEEN-**TOO**-RAH

Pan ....la cacerola
LA KAH-SEH-**ROH**-LAH

Pick ....el pico
EL **PEE**-KOH

Pipe ....el tubo, la pipa, la tubería
EL **TOO**-BOH, LA PEE-PAH, LA
TOO-BEH-**REE**-AH

Pitch fork ....la horca
LA **OR**-KAH

Plaster ....el yeso
EL **YEH**-SOH

Plastic................................el plástico
EL **PLAH**-STEE-KOH

Pliers..................................las tenacillas
LAHS TEH-NAH-**SEE**-YAHS

Plow ....el arado
EL AH-**RAH**-DOH

Plumbing.............................la tubería
LA TOO-BEH-**REE**-AH

Poison ....el veneno
EL VEH-**NEH**-NOH

Pole ....el palo
EL **PAH**-LOH

Pole long ....el palo largo
EL **PAH**-LOH **LAR**-GOH

Post ....el poste
EL **POH**-STEH

Pots ....las ollas
LAHS **OH**-YAHS

Pruning sheers ....las tijeras para podar
LAHS TEE-**HEH**-RAHS **PAH**-RAH
POH-**DAHR**

Pump ....la bomba
                                   LA **BOHM**-BAH

Rag...................................el trapo
                                   EL **TRAH**-POH

Rake ....el rastrillo
                                   EL RAHS-**TREE**-YOH

Railroad ties ....madera de la vía férra
                                   MAH-**DEH**-RAH DEH LAH **VEE**-
                                   AH **FEH**-REAH

Rope ....la cuerda
                                   LA **KOOER**-DAH

Rubber ....la goma
                                   LA **GOH**-MAH

Sand..................................la arena
                                   LA AH-**REH**-NAH

Saw...................................la sierra
                                   LA SEE-**EH**-RAH

Scale ....la báscula
                                   LA **BAHS**-KOO-LAH

Scissors ....las tijeras
                                   LAHS TEE-**HEH**-RAHS

Screw ....el tornillo
                                   EL TOR-**NEE**-YOH

Screwdriver .... el destornillador
EL DES-TOR- NEE-AH-**DOR**

Seeds .... las semillas
LAHS SEH-**MEE**-YAHS

Shovel .... la pala
LA **PAH**-LAH

Round nose .... la pala redondo
LA **PAH**-LAH REH-**DOHN** DAH

Square nose .... la pala cuadrada
LA **PAH**-LAH KOOA-**DRAH**-DAH

Sickle .... la hoz
LA HOOS

Sink .... el albañal
EL AHL-BAH-**NYAL**

Soap .... el jabón
EL HAH-**BOHN**

Soil .... el terreno, la tierra
EL TEHR-**REH**-NOH, LA
TEE-**EH**-RAH

Spade .... la azada
LA AH-**SAH**-DAH

Spark plug .... la bujía
LAH BOO-**HEE**-AH

Sponge.................................la esponja
LA ES-**POHN**-HAH

Spoon.................................la cuchara
LA KOO-**CHAH**-RAH

Sprayer ....la pulverizadora
LA POOL-VEH-REE-SAH-**DOH**-RAH

Spring.................................el resorte
EL REH-**SOR**-REH

Sprinkler ....el rociador
EL ROH-SEE-AH-**DOR**

Stake ....la estaca
LA ES-**TAH**-KAH

Stick ....el palo
EL **PAH**-LOH

Stool ....el taburete
EL TAH-BOO-**REH**-TEH

Supplies ....los provisiones
LOHS PROH-VEE-SEE-**OH**-NEHS

Tank.................................el tanque
EL **TAHN**-KEH

Tape.................................la cinta
LA **SEEN**-TAH

Tape measure........................la cinta para medir
LAH **SEEN**-TAH **PAH**-RAH
MEH-**DEER**

Thermometer ....el termómetro
EL TEHR-**MOH**-MEH-TROH

Tools ....las herramientas
LAHS EHR-AH-MEE-**EHN**-TAHS

Towel ....la toalla
LA TOH-**AL**-YAH

Tractor ....el tractor
EL **TRAK**-TOR

Trash can ....el basurero
EL BAH-SOO-**REH**-ROH

Trays ....las bandejas
LAHS BAHN-**DEH**-HAHS

Trellis................................el enrejado
EL EHN-**REH**-HAH-DOH

Trowel...............................la pala de mano
LA **PAH**-LAH DEH **MAH**-NO

Truck ....el camion
EL KAH-MEE-**OHN**

Valve ....la válvula
LA **VAHL**-VOO-LAH

Valve key ....la llave para la válvula
LA **YAH**-VEH **PAH**-RAH LA
VAHL-VOO-LAH

Water ....el agua
EL **AH**-GUAH

Water tank ....la cisterna
LA SEES-**TEHR**-NAH

Watering can ....la regadera
LA REH-GAH-**DEH**-RAH

Wheel ....la rueda
LA ROO-**EH**-DAH

Wheelbarrow ....la carretilla
LA KAH-REH-**TEE**-YAH

Wire ....el alambre
EL AH-**LAHM**-BREH

Wood ....la madera
LA MAH-**DEH**-RAH

Wrench ....la llave
LA **YAH**-VEH

The Plant Family
General Terms
Bush..................................el arbusto
EL AR-**BOOS**-TOH

Cactus ....el cacto
EL **KAHK**-TOH

Crop ....la cosecha
LA KOH-**SEH**-CHAH

Fern................................el helecho
EL EH-**LEH**-CHO

Forest ....el bosque
EL **BOHS**-KEH

Grass...............................la hierba, el zacate, el césped
LA EE-**EHR**-BAH, EL SAH-**KAH**-
THE, EL **SES**-PED

Hedge ....el seto
EL **SEH**-TOH

Herbs ....las hierbas
LAHS HEE-**EHR**-BAHS

Moss ....el musgo
EL **MOOS**-GOH

Plant ....la planta
LA **PLAHN**-TAH

Shrub ....el arbusto
EL AR-**BOOS**-TOH

Tree................................el arbol
EL **AR**-BOL

Vine.....................................la vid, la enredadera
LAH VEED, LA EN-REH-
DAH-**DEH**-RAH

Weed ....la mala hierba
EL **MAH**-LAH EE-**EHR**-BAH

Woods ....el bosque
EL **BOHS**-KEH

Parts of a Plant or Tree

Bark...................................la corteza
LA KOR-**TEH**-SAH

Berry..................................la baya
LA **BAH**-YAH

Blossom ....la flor
LA FLOR

Branch...............................la rama
LA **RAH**-MAH

Bud....................................el brote
EL **BROH**-TEH

Cane ....la guía
LA **GEE**-AH

Flower ....la flor
LA FLOR

Fruit ....la fruta
LA **FROO**-TAH

Grain.................................el grano
EL **GRAH**-NOH

Leaf ....la hoja

Limb ....la rama
LA **RAH**-MAH

Nut....................................la nuez
LA NOOES

Pollen................................el polen
EL **POH**-LEN

Pulp..................................la pulpa
LA **POOL**-PAH

Root ....la raiz
LA RAH-**EES**

Sap ....la savia
LA **SAH**-VEEAH

Sapling..............................el bástago, el renuevo
EL **BAH**-STAH-GO, EL REH-
NOOEH-VOH

Seed..................................la semilla, la pepita
LA SEH-**MEE**-YAH, LA
PEH-**PEE**-TAH

Seedling ....la planta de semillero, el arbolillo
LA **PLAHN**-TAH DEH SEH-MEE-
YEH-ROH, EL AR-BOHL-**EE**-YOH

Spurs.....................................los espolones, las espuelas
                                          LOHS ES-POH-**LOH**-NEHS, LAHS
                                          ES-POO-**EH**-LAHS

Stalk....................................el tronco
                                          EL **TROHN**-KOH

Sucker ....el chupón
                                          EL CHOO-**POHN**

Trunk ....el tronco
                                          EL **TROHN**-KOH

Twig ....la varita, la ramita
                                          LA VAH-**REE**-TAH, LA
                                          RAH-**MEE**-TAH

Plant Conditions

Budding ....brotando
                                          BROH-**TAHN**-DOH

Dead ....muerto
                                          MOOEHR-TOH

Dying ....muriendo
                                          MOO-REH-**EN**-DOH

Flowering ....floreciendo
                                          FLO-REH-SEE-**EN**-DOH

Growing...............................creciendo
                                          KREH-SEE-**EN**-DOH

Going to seed ....granando
GRAH-**NAHN**-DOH

Healthy ....sano
SAH-NOH

Producing ....produciendo
PRO-DOO-SEE-**EN**-DOH

Rotting ....pudriendo
POO-DREE-**EN**-DOH

Wilting ....marchitando
MAR-CHEE-**TAHN**-DOH

Vegetables

Artichokes ....las alcachofas
LAHS AHL-KAH-**CHOH**-FAHS

Asparagus ....el espárrago
EL EH-**SPAR**-RAH-GOH

Avocado ....el aguacate, la palta
EL AH-GUA-**KAH**-THE, LA
PAHL-TAH

Beans.................................las habas, las habichuelas
LAHS **AH**-BAHS, LAHS
AH-BEE-**CHOOEH**-LAS

Beans green..........................las habichuelas verdes
LAHS AH-BEE-**CHOOEH**-LAS
VEHR-DES

Beans kidney..........................los frijoles rojos
LOHS FREE-**HOH**-LEHS
ROH-HOHS

Beans lima ....Las habas de lima
LAHS **AH**-BAHS DEH **LEE**-MAH

Beans navy ....los frijoles blancos
LOHS FREE-**HOH**-LEHS
BLAHN-KOHS

Beans shell ....los frijoles
LOHS FREE-**HOH**-LEHS

Beans string..........................los elotes, las habichuelas
verdes
LOHS EH-**LOH**-TES, LAHS
AH-BEE-**CHOOEH**-LAHS
VEHR-DEHS

Beans soy.............................las soyas
LAHS **SOH**-YAHS

Beets.................................los betabeles, la remolacha
LOHS BEH-TAH-**BEH**-LEHS, LA
REH-MOH-**LAH**-CHA

Broccoli ....el broccoli, el brécol
EL **BROO**-KOH-LEE, EL
BREH-KOHL

Brussels sprouts.....................la col de Bruselas
LA KOHL DEH BROO-**SEH**-LAHS

Cabbage ....La col el repollo
LAH KOHL EL REH-**POH**-YOH

Cabbage Chinese ....la col de China
LA KOHL DEH **CHEE**-NAH

Carrots ....la zanahoria
LA ZAHN-AH-**OH**-REEAH

Cauliflower ....la coliflor
LA KOH-LEE-**FLOR**

Celery ....el apio
EL **AH**-PEEOH

Chili...................................el chile
EL **CHEE**-LEH

Corn ....el maíz, el grano, el elote
EL MAH-**EES,** EL **GRAH**-NO, EL
EH-**LOH**-TEH

Cucumbers ....los pepinos
LOS PEEH-**PEE**-NOS

Eggplant..............................la berenjena, la planta de huevo
LA BEH-REN-**HEH**-NAH, LA
PLAHN-TAH DEH **OOEH**-VOH

Garlic ....el ajo
EL **AH**-HOH

Leeks ....los puerros
LOHS **POOEH**-ROHS

Lentils ....las lentejas
         LAS LEN-**TEH**-HAS

Lettuce ....la lechuga
         LA LEH-**CHOO**-GAH

Mushrooms ....los hongos
         LOHS **OHN**-GOHS

Olives...............................las aceitunas
         LAHS AH-SEHEE-**TOO**-NAHS

Onions ....las cebollas
         LAHS SEH-**BOH**-YAHS

Parsley..............................el perejil
         EL PEH-REH-**HEEL**

Parsnips ....las chirivías
         LAHS CHEE-REE-**VEE**-AHS

Peas ....los chícharos, las arvejas
         LOHS **CHEE**-CHAH-ROHS, LAHS
         AR-**VEH**-HAHS

Peppers..............................los pimientos
         LOHS PEE-MEE-**EN**-TOS

Potatoes ....las papas, las potatas
         LAHS **PAH**-PAHS, LAHS
         POH-**TAH**-TAS

Pumpkins ....las calabazas
         LAHS KAH-LAH-**BAH**-SAHS

Radishes . . . . los rabanos
LOHS **RAH**-BAH-NOS

Rice . . . . el arroz
EL AH-**ROHS**

Spinach . . . . la espinaca
LA ES-PEE-**NAH**-KAH

Squash . . . . la calabaza
LA KAH-LAH-**BAH**-ZAH

Tomatoes . . . . los tamates
LOHS TOH-**MAH**-TES

Turnips . . . . los nabos
LOHS **NAH**-BOHS

Vegetables . . . . las legumbres, las verduras, los
vegetales
LAHS LEH-**GOOM**-BREHS
LAHS VEHR-**DOO**-RAHS LOHS
VEH-HEH-**TAH**-LEHS

Zucchini . . . . la calabaza
LAH KAH-LAH-**BAH**-SAH

Fruits
Fruit   **Fruit Tree**

Apple	la manzana	el manzano
	LAH MAHN-**SAH**-NAH	EL MAHN-**SAH**-NOH

Apricot	el abaricoque, el chabacano	
	AL AL-BAR-EE-**KOH**-KEH, EL	
	CHAH-BAH-**KAH**-NO	
Banana	el plátano, la banana	el plátano, el banano
	EL **PLAH**-TAH-NO, LA	EL **PLAH**-TAH-NO, EL
	BAH-**NAH**-NAH	BAH-**NAH**-NOH
Cherry	la cereza	el cerezo
	LA SEH-**REH**-SAH	EL SEH-**REH**-SOH
Citrus	el cítrico	
	EL **SEE**-TREE-KOH	
Dates	los dátiles	
	LOHS **DAH**-TEE-LEHS	
Fig	el higo	la higuera
	EL **EE**-GOH	LA EE-**GEH**-RAH
Grapefruit	la toronja	el toronjo
	LA TOH-**ROHN**-HAH	EL TOH-**ROHN**-HOH
Grapes	las uvas	la vid
	LAHS **OO**-VAHS	LA VEED
Grapes, bunch	el racimo de uvas	
	EL RAH-**SEE**-MOH DEH **OO**-VAHS	
Guava	la guayaba	el guayabo
	LA GUAH-**YAH**-BAH	EHL GUAH-**YAH**-BOH

Lemon	el limón	el limonero
	EL LEE-**MOHN**	EL LEE-MOHN-**EH**-ROH

Lime	la lima	
	LA **LEE**-MAH	

Melon	el melón	
	EL MEH-**LOHN**	

Mango	el mango	
	EL **MAHN**-GOH	

Necatarine	el abridor, el liso	
	EL AH-BREE-**DOHR**, EL **LEE**-SO	

Orange	la naranja	el naranjo
	LA NAR-**AHN**-HAH	EL NAR-**AHN**-HOH

Peach	el durazno, el melocotón	el duraznero, el meloncotonero
	EL DOO-**RAHS**-NO, EL MEH-LOH-KOH-**TOHN**	EL DOO-RAHS-**NEH**-ROH, EL MEH-LOH-KOH-TOH-**NEH**-ROH

Pear	la pera	el peral
	LA **PEH**-RAH	EL PEH-**RAHL**

Pineapple	la piña	
	LA **PEE**-NYAH	

Plum	la ciruela	el ciruelo
	LA SEE-**ROOEH**-LAH	EL SEE-**ROOEH**-LOH

Pomegranate   la granada
              LA GRAH-**NAH**-DAH

Prune   la ciruela seca
              LA SEE-**ROOEH**-LAH
              SEH-KAH

Raisins   las pasas
              LAHS **PAH**-SAHS

Tangerine   la tanerina
              LA TAHN-EH-**REE**-NAH

Watermelon   la sandía
              LA SAHN-**DEE**-AH

Berries

Cranberry............................el grandano agrio
              EL GRAHN-**DAH**-NO **AH**-GREEOH

Berry.................................la baya
              LA **BAH**-YAH

Blackberry ....la zarzamora
              LA SAR-SAH-**MOH**-RAH

Blueberry ....la mora azul
              LA **MOH**-RAH AH-**SOOL**

Boysenberry ....variedad de la zarzamora
              VAH-REE-EH-**DAD** DEH LAH
              SAR-SAH-**MOH**-RAH

Mulberry............................la mora
LA **MOH**-RAH

Mulberry tree.......................la morera
LA MOH-**REH**-RAH

Raspberry............................la frambuesa
LA FRAHM-**BOOEH**-SAH

Strawberry...........................la fresa
LA **FREH**-SAH

Nuts

Nut		Nut Tree
Almond	la almendra	el almendro
	LA AHL-**MEHN**-DRAH	EL AHL-**MEHN**-DROH
Brazil nut	nuez de Brazíl	
	NOOES DEH	
	BRAH-**SEEL**	
Cashew	el anacardo	el anacardo
	EL AHN-AH-**KAR**-DOH	EL AHN-AH-**KAR**-DOH
Chestnut	la castaña	el castaño
	LA KAHS-**TAH**-NYA	EL KAHS-**TAH**-NYO
Hazelnut	la avellana	el avellano
	LA AH-VEH-**YAH**-NAH	EL AH-VEH-**YAH**-NOH
Macadamia	Same as english	

Pecan	la pacana	el pacana
	LA PAH-**KAH**-NAH	EL PAH-**KAH**-NAH
Walnut	el nogal	la noguera
	EHL NOH-**GAHL**	LAH NOH-**GEH**-RAH

Common Trees

Ash .... el fresno
EL **FRES**-NO

Birch .... el abudel
EL AH-BEH-**DOOL**

Elm .... el olmo
EL **OHL**-MOH

Eucalyptus .... el eucalipto
EL EH-OO-KAH-**LEEP**-TOH

Maple .... el arce
EL **AR**-SEH

Oak .... el roble
EL **ROH**-BLEH

Olive .... el olivo
EL OH-**LEE**-VOH

Palm .... la plamera
LA PAHL-**MEH**-RAH

Pine .... el pino
EL **PEE**-NOH

Other Crops

Alfalfa...............................la alfalfa
LA AHL-**FAHL**-FAH

Cotton..............................el algodón
EL AHL-GOH-**DOHN**

Barley...............................la cebada
LA SEH-**BAH**-DAH

Herbs ....las hierbas
LAHS HEE-**EHR**-BAHS

Oats..................................la avena
LA AH-**VEH**-NAH

Peanuts ....las cacahuates, la maní
LAHS KAH-KAH-**HOOAH**-TEHS,
LA MAH-**NEE**

Rice ....el arroz
EL AH-**ROHS**

Tobacco ....el tabaco
EL TAH-**BAH**-KOH

Wheat ....el trigo
EL **TREE**-GOH

Land and Soil Terminology

Acre..................................el acre
EL **AH**-KREH

Clay ....la arcilla
                LA AR-**SEE**-YAH

Clod ....el terrón
                EH TEH-**ROHN**

Ditch.................................la zanja
                LA **SAHN**-HAH

Dirt ....la tierra
                LA TEE-**EH**-RAH

Earth.................................la tierra
                LA TEE-**EH**-RAH

Earthworms ....las lombrices de tierra
                LAHS LOHM-**BREE**-SEHS DEH
                TEE-**EH**-RAH

Furrow ....el surco
                EL **SIR**-KOH

Ground..............................la tierra
                LA TEE-**EH**-RAH

Hardpan.............................La capa dura
                LA **KAH**-PAH **DOO**-RAH

Hill ....la colima
                LA KOH-**LEE**-MAH

Humus.................................el humas
                EL **OO**-MOHS

Mud....................................el barro, el lodo
EL **BAR**-ROH, EL **LOH**-DOH

Plot ....el pedazo de terreno
EL PEH-**DAH**-SOH DEH
TEH-**REH**-NOH

Property ....la propiedad
LA PRO-PEE-EH-**DAHD**

Slope (bank) ....el sesgo
EL **SEHS**-GOH

Soil...................................el suelo, el terreno, la
tierra
EL **SOOEH**-LOH, EL TEHR-**REH**-
NO, LA TEE-**EH**-RAH

Animals Insects Birds and Other Creatures

Aphids ....las áfidos
LOHS **AH**-FEE-DOHS

Ants..................................las hormigas
LAHS OR-**MEE**-GAHS

Ant Hill ....el hormiguero
EL OR-MEE-**GEH**-ROH

Bees..................................las abejas
LAHS AH-**BEH**-HAHS

Beehive ....la colmena
LA KOHL-**MEH**-NAH

Beetles.................................los escarabajos
                                         LOHS ES-KAR-AH-**BAH**-
                                         HOHS

Birds ....los aves, los pájaros
                                         LOHS **AH**-VEHS, LOHS
                                         PAH-HAH-ROHS

Bugs...................................las chinches, las sabandijas
                                         LAHS **CHEEN**-CHEHS, LAHS
                                         SAH-BAHN-**DEE**-HAHS

Butterfly.............................la mariposa
                                         LA MAH-REE-**POH**-SAH

Bull....................................el toro
                                         EL **TOH**-ROH

Calf ....el becerro
                                         EL BEH-**SEH**-ROH

Cat ....el gato
                                         EL **GAH**-TOH

Chickens ....los pollos
                                         LOHS **POH**-YOHS

Chick ....el pollito
                                         EL POH-**YEE**-TOH

Cockroach ....la cucaracha
                                         LA KOO-KAH-**RAH**-CHA

Colt ....el potro
                                         EL **POH**-TROH

Cow . . . . la vaca
LA **VAH**-KAH

Coyote . . . . el coyote
EL KOH-**YOH**-TEH

Grasshoppers . . . . los saltamontes
LOHS SAHL-TAH-**MOHN**-TEHS

Hen . . . . la gallina
LAH GAH-**YEE**-NAH

Horse . . . . el caballo
EL KAH-**BAH**-YOH

Insects . . . . los insectos
LOHS EEN-**SEK**-TOHS

Ladybugs . . . . las mariquitas
LAHS MAH-REE-**KEE**-TAHS

Lamb . . . . el cordero
EL KOR-**DEH**-ROH

Livestock . . . . el ganado
EL GAH-**NAH**-DOH

Lizard . . . . el lagarto
EL LAH-**GAR**-TOH

Mice . . . . los ratones
LOHS RAH-**TOH**-NEHS

Moles . . . . los topos
LOHS **TOH**-POHS

Mosquito . . . . el mosquito
EL MOH-**SKEE**-TOH

Deer . . . . el venado
EL VEH-**NAH**-DOH

Dog . . . . el perro
EL **PEH**-ROH

Donkey . . . . el burro
EL **BOO**-ROH

Duck . . . . el pato
EL **PAH**-TOH

Eagle . . . . el águila
EL **AHG**-EE-LAH

Flies . . . . las mosacas
LAHS **MOHS**-KAHS

Fox . . . . el zorro
EL **SOH**-ROH

Frog . . . . la rana
LA **RAH**-NAH

Goat . . . . la cabra
LAH **KAH**-BRAH

Goose . . . . el ganso
EL **GAHN**-SOH

Gophers . . . . los roedores
LOHS ROH-EH-**DOR**-EHS

Mule ....el mulo
EL **MOO**-LOH

Pig.....................................el cerdo, el puerco
EL **SEHR**-DOH, EL **POOER**-KOH

Poultry ....los aves de corral
LOHS **AH**-VEHS DEH KOH-
RAHL

Rabbits ....los conejos
LOHS KOH-**NEH**-HOHS

Rattlesnake ....la culebra de cascabel
LA KOO-**LEH**-BRAH DEH
KAHS-KAH-**BELL**

Rooster.............................el gallo
EL **GAH**-YOH

Sheep ....la oveja
LA OH-**VEH**-HAH

Slugs ....las babosas
LAHS BAH-**BOH** SAHS

Snails................................los caracoles
LOHS KAHR-AH-**KOH**-LEHS

Snake ....la culabra, la vípora
LAH KOO-**LAH**-BRAH, LA
VEE-POH-RAH

Spider...............................la araña
LA AH-**RAH**-NYAH

Squirrel.................................la ardilla
                                                    LA AR-**DEE**-YAH

Termites...............................las termitas
                                                    LAHS TEHR-**MEE**-TAHS

Toad.....................................el sapo
                                                    EL **SAH**-POH

Turkey ....el pavo
                                                    EL **PAH**-VOH

Turtle ....la tortuga
                                                    LA TOR-**TOO**-GAH

Wolf ....el lobo
                                                    EL **LOH**-BOH

Wasps..................................las avispas
                                                    LAHS AH-**VEES**-PAHS

Worms ....los lombrices
                                                    LOHS LOHM-**BREE**-SEHS

Weather Climate and Outdoor Terminology

Air.......................................el aire
                                                    AL **AHEE**-REH

Breeze ....la brisa
                                                    LA **BREE**-SAH

Brush ....el breñal
                                                    EL BREH-**NYAL**

Clouds...............................las nubes
LAHS NOO-**BEHS**

Cloudy..............................nublado
NOO-**BLAH**-DOH

Cold ....frío
FREE-YOH

Cool ....fresco
FRES-KOH

Dew.................................el rocío
EL ROH-**SEE**-OH

Drought ....la sequedad
LA SEH-KEH-**DAD**

Dry.................................seco
SEH-KOH

Dust................................el polvo
EL **POHL**-VOH

Fog ....la niebla
LA NEE-**EH**-BLAH

Foggy ....nebuloso
NEH-BOO-**LOH**-SOH

(to) freeze...........................helar
EH-**LAR**

Frost ....la escarcha
                                        LA ES-**KAR**-CHAH

Hail ....el granizo
                                        EL GRAH-**NEE**-SOH

Heat..................................el calor
                                        EL **KAH**-LOR

Humid ....húmedo
                                        OO-MEH DOH

Hurricane ....el huracán
                                        EL OO-RAH-**KAHN**

Lightening ....el relámpago
                                        EL REH-**LAHM**-PAH-GOH

Moon ....la luna
                                        LA **LOO**-NAH

Nature ....la natureleza
                                        LA NAH-TOO-REH-**LEH**-SAH

Rain ....la lluvia
                                        LA **YOO**-VEEAH

Rainy.................................lluvioso
                                        YOO-**VEEOH**-SO

Shade ....la sombra
                                        LA **SOHM**-BRAH

Sky ....el cielo
EL SEE-**EH**-LOH

Sleet ....la aguanieve
LA AH-GOOAH-NEE-**EH**-VEH

Snow....................................la nieve
LA NEE-**EH**-VEH

(to) snow.............................nevar
NEH-**VAR**

Storm..................................la tormenta
LA TOR-**MEN**-TAH

Stormy ....tempestuoso
TEM-PES-TOO-**OH**-SO

Sun ....el sol
EL SOHL

Sunny ....asoleado
AH-SOH-LEH-**AH**-DOH

Thunder..............................el trueno
EL TROO-**EH**-NO

Water ....el agua
EL **AH**-GUAH

Weather ....el tiempo
EL TEE-**EHM**-POH

Weather Forecast .... el prognóstico del tiempo
EL PROG-**NOS**-TEE-KOH DEL
TEE-**EHM**-POH

Wet .... mohado
MOH-**AH**-DOH

Wind................................... el viento
EL VEE-**EN**-TOH

Windy .... ventoso
VEN-**TOH**-SO

It's hot (cold). .... Hace calor (frío).
AH-SEH KAH-**LOR** (**FREE**-OH).

Marketing and Money

Bill .... el billete
EL BEE-**YEH**-TEH

Box................................... la caja
LA **KAH**-HAH

Buyer .... el comprador
EL KOHM-PRAH-**DOR**

Cash................................... dinero efectivo
DEH-**NEH**-ROH
EH-FEK- **TEE**-VOH

Cents .... centavos
SEN-**TAH**-VOHS

Change .... el cambio
EL **KAHM**-BEEOH

Customer ....el cliente
EL KLEE-**EN**-TEH

Dollars ....dólares
DOH-LAH-REHS

Free of Charge ....gratis
GRAH-TEES

Loss ....la pérdida
LA **PEHR**-DEE-DAH

Market...............................el mercado
EL MEHR-**KAH**-DOH

Money ....el dinero
EL DEE-**NEH**-ROH

Packer ....el (la) empaquetador (a)
EL (LA) EM-PAH-KEH-TAH-**DOR**
(**DOH**-RAH)

Packing House ....la casa de empaque
LA **KAH**-SAH DEH EM- **PAH**-
KEH

Price ....el precio
EL **PREH**-SEEOH

Produce ....el producto
EL PRO-**DOOK**-TOR

Produce Stand......................puesto de verduras
POOES-TOH DEH
VEHR-**DOO**-RAHS

Profit ....la ganacia
                                    LA GAH-**NAHN**-SEEAH

Receipt ....el recibo
                                    EL REH-**SEE**-BOH

Sale...................................la venta
                                    LA **VEN**-TAH

Scale ....la báscula
                                    LA **BAHS**-KOO-LAH

Seller ....el vendedor
                                    EL VEN-DEH-**DOR**

Weight...............................el peso
                                    EL **PEH**-SO

Warehouse..........................el almacén, el depósito
                                    EL AHL-MAH-**SEN,** EL
                                    DEH-**POH**-SEE-TOH

Descriptive Words
Large.................................grande
                                    GRAHN-DEH

Larger ....más grande
                                    MAHS **GRAHN**-DEH

Small.................................pequeño
                                    PEH-**KEH**-NYOH

Smaller ....más pequeño
                                    MAHS PEH-**KEH**-NYOH

Deep .... hondo, profundo
PROH-**FOON**-DOH, **OHN**-
DOH

Shallow .... poco profundo
POH-KOH PROH-**FOON**-DOH

Good .... bueno
BOOEH-NO

Bad .... malo
MAH-LOH

Strong .... fuerte
FOOEHR-TEH

Weak .... debil
DEH-BEEL

Wide .... ancho
AHN-CHO

Narrow .... estrecho, angosto
ES-**TREH**-CHO, AHN-**GO**-
STOH

Long .... largo
LAR-GO

Short .... corto
KOR-TOH

High (tall) .... alto
AHL-TOH

Low (short)...........................bajo
                                    BAH-HOH

Easy ....fácil
                                    FAH-SEEL

Difficult ....dificil
                                    DEE-**FEE**-SEEL

Hard ....duro
                                    DOO-ROH

Soft...................................blando
                                    BLAHN-DOH

Pretty...............................bonito
                                    BOH-**NEE**-TOH

Ugly..................................feo
                                    FEE-OH

Light ....ligero, liviano
                                    LEE-**HEH**-ROH, LEE-VEE-**AH**-NO

Heavy................................pesado
                                    PEH-**SAH**-DOH

Thin..................................Flaco, delgado
                                    FLAH-KOH, DEL-**GAH**-DOH

Thick ....grueso
                                    GROOEH-SOH

Straight ....derecho
DEH-**REH**-CHO, **REK**-TOH

Crooked..............................torcido
TOR-**SEE**-DOH

Before ....antes
AHN-TES

After ....después
DEHS-**POOEHS**

All......................................todo
TOH-DOH

None..................................ninguno
NEEN-**GOO**-NO

Alive ....vivo
VEE-VOH

Dead ....muerto
MOOEHR-TOH

Round ....redondo
REH-**DOHN**-DOH

Flat.....................................plano
PLAH-NO

Big......................................grande
GRAHN-DEH

Little .... pequeño
PEH-**KEH**-NYOH

Rough .... áspero
TOS-KOH **AH**-SPEH-ROH

Smooth .... llano, liso
YAH-NO, **LEE**-SO

Locational Words

Across .... de través, a través de
DEH TRAH-**VEHS,** AH TRAH-
VEHS DE

Over .... sobre, encima
EN-**SEE**-MAH **SOH**-BREH

Under................................... debajo de
DEH-**BAH**-HOH DEH

Down .... abajo
AH-**BAH**-HOH

Up..................................... arriba
AH-**REE**-BAH

Inside .... dentro de
DEN-TROH DEH

Outside............................... fuera de, afuera
FOOEH-RAH DEH,
AH-**FOOEH**-RAH

Next to ....al lado
AHL **LAH**-DOH

Left...................................izquierdo
EES-**KEEHR**-DOH

Right.................................derecho
DEH-**REH**-CHOH

Behind ....átras de, detrás
AH-**TRAS DEH,** DEH-**TRAHS**

Away.................................fuera
FOOEH-RAH

In Front of ....en frente de, delante
EHN **FREHN**-TEH DEH,
DEH-**LAHN**-TEH

Forward ....adelante
AH-DEH-**LAHN**-TEH

Backward ....atras de
AH-**TRAHS** DEH

Backwards ....al reves
AHL REH-**VEHS**

Under................................abajo, debajo
AH-**BAH**-HOH, DEH-**BAH**-HOH

Over ....sobre
SOH-BREH

Anywhere .... en cualquier parte
EN KOO-AHL-KEEHR PAR-TEH

Nowhere .... el ninguna parte
EN **NEEN**-GOON **PAR**-TEH

Before .... antes
AHN-TES

After .... después
DEHS-**POOEHS**

Above .... encima
EN-**SEE**-MAH

Below .... abajo, debajo
AH-**BAH**-HOH, DEH-
BAH-HOH

Next .... el próximo, siguiente
EL **PROH**-KSEE-MOH,
SEEG-**EEHN**-TEH

Beside .... al lado
AHL **LAH**-DOH

Around .... alrededor
AHL-REH-DEH-**DOR**

Last .... último
OOL-TEE-MOH

First .... primero
PREE-**MEH**-ROH

Cardinal Points

North .... norte
NOR-TEH

South .... sur, sud
SOOD, SOOHR

East .... este
ES-TEH

West .... oeste
OH-**ES**-TEH

Amounts

A Bunch of .... racimo
RAH-**SEE**-MOH

All .... todo
TOH-DOH

A Lot of .... mucho
MOO-CHO

Many .... muchos
MOO-CHOS

None .... ninguno
NEEN-**GOO**-NO

A Few .... pocos
POH-KOS

Some .... algunos
AHL-**GOO**-NOS

Miscellaneous Words

And ....y
EE

But ....pero
PEH-ROH

Each every ....cado uno
KAH-DAH **OOH**-NO

Anything ....cualquier cosa
KOOAHL- KEEHR **KOH**- SAH

Nothing ....nada
NAH-DAH

Yes....................................si
SEE

No.....................................no
NO

This ....este, esta, esto
EHS-TAH **EHS**-TOH **EHS**-TEH

That..................................este, esa, eso
EH-SAH **EH**-SOH **EH**-SEH

These ....estas, estos
EHS-TAHS **EHS**-TOHS

Those ....aquellas, aquellos
AH-**KEH**-YAHS AH-**KEH**-YOHS

Verbs

Able (to be)	poder
Accept	aceptar
Ache	doler
Adjust	ajustar
Afraid (to lose)	tener, miedo
Apply	aplicar
Ask	preguntar
Attach	ligar, adherir
Be	ser estar
Begin	empezar
Bite	morder
Bloom	florecer
Break	romper, quebrar
Bring	traer
Brush	cepillar
Build	construer, edificar
Burn	quemar
Bury	enterrar
Buy	comprar
Call	llamar
Care for	cuidar
Carry	llevar, cargar
Carry away	llevarse
Clean	limpiar
Clear	aclarar, despejar
Climb	subir
Close	cerrar
Collect	recojer, juntar
Come	venir
Connect	conectar
Cost	costar
Count	contar
Cover	cubrir, tapar

Cross	atravesar
Cull	escojer, selectionar
Cultivate	cultivar
Cut	cortar
Defoliate	deshojar
Deliver	entregar
Detach	separar
Dig	Cavar, escavar
Dig up	desenterrar
Distribute	distribuir, repartir
Do	hacer
Drink	beber tomar
Drip	gotear
Drive	manejar, conducir
Drop	bajar, dejar, caer
Dry	secar
Earn	ganar
Eat	comer
Employ	emplear
Enter	entrar
Explain	explicar
Fall	caer
Feed	alimentar
Fertilize	fertilizer, fecundar
Find	encontrar
Finish	terminar
Fix	arreglar
Fold	doblar
Follow	seguir
Forget	olvidar
Gain	ganar
Gather	amontar, juntar
Give	dar

Graft	injertar
Grow	brotar, crecer, cultivar
Hang	colgar
Hear	oir
Help	ayudar
Hide	esconder
Hire	arrendar, contratar
Hitch	acoplar
Hoe	acodonar, enganchar
Hold	sostener, detener
Hunt	cazar
Hurt	dañar
Improve	mejorar
Inspect	inspeccionar
Irrigate	regar, irrigar
Jump	saltar
Keep	guarder, mantener
Kill	matar
Know	saber
Learn	aprendar
Leave	salir
Leave something	dejar
Let lift	permitir
Listen	levantar
Live	vivir
Load	cargar
Lock	cerrar
Look	mirar
Lose	perder
Lubricate	lubricar
Maintain	mantener
Make	hacer
Make (to make a)	producir

Measure	medir
Mix	mezclar
Mow	segar, cortar
Nail	clavar
Need	necesitar
Obtain	obtener
Oil	aceitear
Pack	empaquetar
Paint	pintar
Park	estacionar
Pay	pagar
Pick	Escojer, elejir
Plant	plantar
Plow	arar
Pollinate	polinizar
Pour	echar
Practice	practicar
Prepare	preparar
Produce	producer
Prune	podar, recortar
Pull	tirar sacar
Pull out	arrancar
Pull down	jalar
Push	empujer
Quit	dejar, parar
Quit work	dejar de trabajar
Rake	rastrillar
Reach	alcanzar
Read	leer
Receive	recibir
Regulate	regular
Remember	acordarse de recordar
Remove	quitar el iminar
Rent	alquilar

Repair	reparar
Request	pedir, requerir
Rest	descansar
Return	devolver
Rot	pudirse
Run	correr
Save	ahorrar
Say	decir
Sell	vender
Send	mandar, enviar
Separate	separar
Shake	sacudir
Sleep	dormir
Smoke	fumar
Sort	separar
Spray	pulverizar
Spread	propagar
Sprinkle	rociar
Stake	estacar
Start	empezar
Sting	picar
Stop	parar
Sweat	sudar
Sweep	borrar
Take	tomar
Talk	hablar, charlar
Tear	romper
Tie	atar
Touch	tocar
Tow	remolcar
Turn	volver
Unload	descargar
Unlock	abrir
Use	usar

Wait	esperar
Walk	andar, caminar
Want	querer, desear
Wash	lavar
Watch	observar mirar
Water	regar
Weed	sacar la mala hierba
Weigh	pesar
Wet	mojar
Wilt	marchitarse
Work	trabajar

Notes

_____

_____

_____

_____

_____

_____

_____

_____

_____

_____

_____

_____

_____

_____

_____

_____

For more information about

- Products

or

- Discounts

Please Contact Us:
Toll Free: 1-800-633-5544
Fax: 760-451-2096
Email: customerservice@ammieenterprises.com

We look forward to serving you.

Ammie Enterprises
P.O. Box 151
Fallbrook, CA 92088-0151
www.ammieenterprises.com

Other Ammie Enterprises Publications...

- A Bilingual Dictionary of School Terminology
- Reporting to Parents in English and Spanish
- School Letters in English and Spanish
- School Office Spanish
- School Terminology Handbook
- Spanish for the School Nurse's Office

Try our Ammie Super Bundle, the complete collection of books used to collaborate with parents to increase quality education for all students while acquiring the skills they need to reach their potential. The bundle contains all six titles of the above titles at 14% off.

Attractively designed, healthy and well-maintained lawns, gardens, and grounds create a positive first impression. A well establish a peaceful mood will undoubtedly increase property values. Gardening in Spanish helps you to communicate with grounds maintenance workers to perform the variety of tasks necessary to achieve a pleasant and functional outdoor environment. With Gardening In Spanish you get the necessary phrases to communicate with your Spanish-speaking employees even if you have no prior knowledge of Spanish. The book features vital words and phrases specific to the gardening and landscaping fields, with translations spelled out phonetically so you can say what you need to right away. From interviewing potential employees to discussing wages and every subject in between, Gardening In Spanish is perfect for learning English too.

Made in the USA
Middletown, DE
19 February 2021

34064138R00075